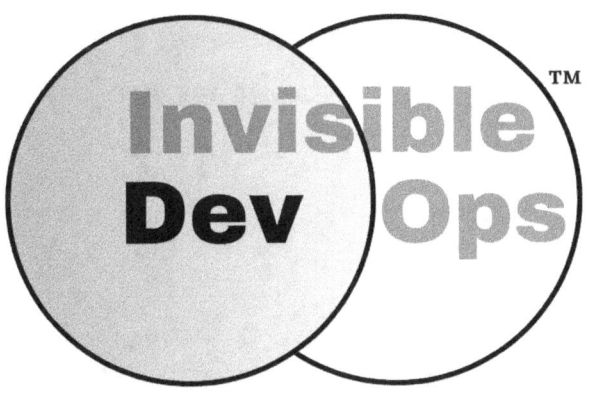

Invisible DevOps™

A system for implementing
DevOps as an invisible culture

by Keith Minkler

Table of Contents

Why Invisible DevOps

The DevOps mindset was born in 2009 when Flickr gave a talk at the O'Reilly Velocity Conference. They described how their Dev and Ops teams cooperated to achieve 10+ deployments per day. While most of us were struggling to deploy code more than once a week, Flickr unveiled a new paradigm of cooperation between traditional development and operations teams.

Since 2009, countless software development organizations have been trying to adopt the same practices and principles that gave Flickr such success. In 2023, Puppet released their annual State of DevOps report. In it they reported that **82% of organizations are still struggling** to achieve high success with DevOps.

I have been a DevOps consultant since 2012. I have seen first hand the exact struggles that are outlined in the State of DevOps report. The struggle is real, but the problems are quite common and shared among organizations working to implement DevOps principles. **You are not alone**!

There is one pattern that I've seen and that is also called out in the State of DevOps report: The organizations who do well at implementing DevOps have stopped calling it DevOps. Instead it's become "the way we do things", a company culture.

Walking into one of these organizations, you won't find a "DevOps team", you won't find any "DevOps Engineers". DevOps isn't another siloed function in these organizations--DevOps is Invisible there. DevOps has become a part of the company culture and values. It's the way of doing things that is ingrained into every employee.

This is why I've written this book, *Invisible DevOps™* to provide organizations and developers a system to get to the next level in their DevOps culture adoption.

If you are a relatively new organization or startup and you haven't yet hired a DevOps Engineer or Sysadm this book will save you time and money. The *Invisible DevOps* system will allow you to delay hiring a DevOps Engineer for some time and will instead help get your development team comfortable with DevOps concepts and principles.

If your organization is more established and you already have several development teams and a DevOps team, this book will show you how to best use these teams to achieve maximum performance and speed of delivery.

This book will show you the secrets of high performing software development teams. The *Invisible DevOps* system provides a framework of components that can be implemented by small and large teams alike.

This book provides teams of all sizes a roadmap for planning future growth. They will know when it's the right time to hire for DevOps skills and not hire too early. A scorecard is provided to evaluate your DevOps adoption success and make adjustments to perform even better.

Let's take that journey together!

Invisible DevOps

Part I
DevOps Culture

Invisible DevOps

1 - The DevOps Mindset

The DevOps mindset is not a new concept. While Flikr coined the term in 2009, DevOps is nothing more than Lean Manufacturing principles applied to software development teams. Lean manufacturing principles have been around since at least the 1930s.

Software development has very little resemblance to car manufacturing assembly lines, however the flow theory still applies. Developers are delivering value to the customer through streams of process and steps. These steps can be inspected and optimized for better flow of value to the customer.

There are 8 components to the DevOps Mindset: Respecting People, Continuous Improvement, Optimize the Whole, Focus on Customers, Enhance Learning, Empower your Team, Increase Flow, and Build Quality In.

These are all Lean principles which are applied to the work of software development in teams. Many of these principles are shared with Agile software development.

Throughout this book, I will assume that your organization is already following an Agile development process. Some of these principles will look familiar, since Agile also pulls from Lean thinking.

Respecting People

Your company is made up of people. People do the work and people manage the people. Respecting people is a DevOps principle that underlies everything else. You cannot implement DevOps well in an organization that is not psychologically safe to work in.

DevOps requires experimentation and some failures along the way to be successful in the end. The organization needs to foster an environment of psychological safety for its employees. Employees need to feel safe to make mistakes and learn from them. Making mistakes is a form of training.

The 2001 *Toyota Way* document describes it this way:

> "We view errors as opportunities for learning.

Rather than blaming individuals, the organization takes corrective actions and distributes knowledge about each experience broadly.

Learning is a continuous company-wide process as superiors motivate and train subordinates; as predecessors do the same for successors; and as team members at all levels share knowledge with one another."

"Safety [at Toyota] includes more than just physical safety; it also means feeling safe psychologically. This starts with a respectful environment where team members do not fear psychological abuse."

Having a DevOps culture means having a culture where it is safe to admit mistakes and failures. A culture where mistakes are seen as opportunities to improve the quality of the process.

Teams need a safe space to discuss their process and issues together. Teams can only function well if there is a high level of trust among the team. A company culture of blaming, shaming, and hiding mistakes is a toxic culture that will struggle to adopt Agile and DevOps mindsets.

Continuous Improvement

Once there is a safe environment to work in, organizations can begin to embrace the principle of Continuous Improvement.

Continuous Improvement means that we must always be willing to challenge our assumptions and the status quo if they are holding back the delivery of value to the customer.

The primary mission of the organization is to deliver value to the customer. Anything and anything that stands in the way of that mission needs to be evaluated and potentially improved.

Improvements must be based on measurable empirical evidence. We can't improve something that we can't measure. In order to implement this mindset we need to open up our processes to the entire company to be visible and inspectable and measurable.

I will go into this in more detail in Chapter 3 where I cover Continuous Improvement using the Plan-Do-Check-Act cycle as an example framework. Bad metrics to use are ones that are trying to measure "team performance" such as story points delivered, lines of code, etc. Developers are smart people who can easily game these metrics to look good.

Better metrics look at the system as a whole such as lead time, cycle time, or defect escape rate.

Optimize the Whole

This leads into the next principle. As an organization we're looking to optimize the whole process. Everything from gathering requirements to development to deployment to operations and eventual decommission.

We must visualize the flow of features from customer conversations all the way to delivering value. This is called the value delivery pipeline. Software deployment is an important part of this that many teams struggle with, but it is only part of the whole value pipeline.

The primary driver of pipeline improvement is automation. Following Agile practices, the organization needs to deliver value to the customer as safely and as frequently as possible. This allows for quicker customer feedback to drive the process forward. I will go into detail about the value delivery pipeline in Chapter 7.

Focus on Customers

I've mentioned customers already, but it's worth elaborating further. The DevOps mindset has a relentless focus on the customers and delivering value to the customer.

The organization needs to cut out any waste in this process and remain laser focused on delivering value to the customer. The art of DevOps is to deliver value as simply as possible. As the Agile Manifesto states:

> Simplicity – the art of maximizing the amount of work not done – is essential

DevOps is not about implementing continuous integration, or using Jenkins, or building elaborate automations. Instead, it's about removing waste and optimizing the process for maximum delivery of value to the customer.

This is not a relentless pursuit of automation, just for the sake of automation. Instead, this is a pursuit of simplicity and efficiency. For example, consider a yearly reconciliation process that is manual and annoying but only takes 20 minutes per year and is difficult to automate. Does it make sense to create an automation project and spend months on automating a difficult process? Probably not, because the time spent in automation will never justify the time saved doing the manual process.

On the other hand, the manual process might be complicated and prone to errors; It might frequently harm the company's reputation and annoy the customers. In this case it may be worthwhile to spend the effort. All of these decisions are tradeoffs that need to be considered in the context of serving the customer, and optimizing the whole.

Focusing on the customer also means understanding what the customer actually wants. This is why it's necessary to have an optimized value delivery pipeline. We need to get the features in front of the customer as quickly as possible so that we can get continual feedback from the customer and improve the product.

This allows us to experiment rapidly, use the customer feedback to improve the product and the pipeline itself.

Enhance Learning

Agile and DevOps teams are small self-organizing and self-managing teams. The team has all the skills and tools necessary to deliver their stream of value to the customer. Sometimes these teams are so isolated from other teams that they are not learning from each other.

A DevOps culture is one where the organization seeks to spread learning and knowledge across the organization rather than contain it within silos.

Teams should be meeting together to share learning and experiences that can help all the teams improve their quality and delivery.

For example, Spotify has many small development teams they call "squads". Within each squad there are many skill sets represented, such as front-end, back-end, database, quality, etc. Spotify groups team members with like skillsets together into Chapters. A front-end development chapter will have front-end developers from a number of squads.

These chapters will meet regularly to share lessons learned, best practices, and helpful tools they've discovered to make development easier. This visibility into the workings of other teams helps each team to grow and improve.

If your organization is large with many teams, such Chapters can help to bring the teams together and share learning. Chapters should be organized around each of the phases of development: Plan, Code, Build, Test, Deploy, Operate, and Monitor.

Chapters are also great places to share learning from experiments which are run in each team.

Empower Your Team

Agile and DevOps teams are said to be self-organizing and self-managing, but what does that mean, really?

Traditional management is based on command and control structures. Orders come from the top down and permission is asked for up the chain of command. This model is slow moving and forces decisions to be made at the top, farthest away from the tactical information at the bottom.

Agile and DevOps teams are different. They are empowered to be self-managing. The management team manages by intent instead of by command. Company Values and Vision are communicated to the teams. The team is then told "what" value they need to deliver to the customer and "why" it is important. The team is then empowered to determine "how" it will be delivered since they are closest to the information necessary to make such decisions.

The team is the smallest unit of ownership in DevOps. Every component in the system must be owned by a single team. A team may own multiple components, but each component has a single team owner.

That team must have all of the skills and knowledge to work on that component and support the component in the production environment. It's up to the team, however, to determine exactly how they want to accomplish their goal.

Management's job is to ensure that the teams have all the tools and training they need to be successful. Different teams may have different needs for tools depending on the component they are working with. Where possible, when there are many teams, management can work with the teams to standardize on a small set of tools to keep costs down.

When an organization has multiple teams, those teams should have a low amount of communication between the teams. This communication is generally related to one team being a dependency of the other. The dependency team should be providing good APIs and documentation for the dependent team in order to limit communication.

Teams will generally not have other teams working on their component of the system. This creates a high amount of communication between teams and causes bottlenecks.

If this sort of collaboration is required from time to time, the dependency team might choose to function as an "internal open source" component. They can accept pull requests from other teams to add functionality to their component. These pull requests must meet the quality standards of the accepting team. Once the team accepts the pull requests, they now own and support the new changes added by the other team.

To adopt the DevOps mindset, the team needs to be empowered owners of the components of the system that they work on. They need to have the organizational safety to experiment when necessary to improve the product. They must have the authority to make decisions that are focused on delivering customer value and are consistent with the values of the organization.

Increase Flow

DevOps is a culture of Lean thinking. Lean thinking is concerned with value flow. The end goal of focusing on delivering customer value, continuous improvement, and optimizing the whole is to increase the speed at which value is delivered to the customer.

We need to visualize the entire process and monitor it with metrics that will indicate areas for improvement. We need to experiment with different processes and measure the results. We need to deliver value as fast and as safely as we can.

Why are we in such a rush? DevOps is a culture that welcomes change. The only thing that is constant in a software development organization is that the product will constantly be changing. New features are always added and old features are modified as we learn more about how the customer interacts with our product.

The DevOps organization needs to welcome and embrace change. The architecture needs to be agile and adapt easily to changing designs and requirements. New components need to be easily added. Whenever it is difficult to make a change the organization needs to ask why.

Increasing flow is not just about developing or deploying faster. It's really about responding to the customer's changing needs. Every customer's interaction with the product will change over time and the organization needs to be able to quickly respond to those changes and deliver new value.

The product owner needs to be willing to cut items from the backlog in response to feedback and learning and potentially move in a new direction. There needs to be some forward looking experimentation done with the customer to anticipate their future needs while also meeting their current needs.

If it takes a long time to respond to a customer request (lead time), then the system as a whole needs to be inspected to determine how to increase flow and deliver value faster.

Build Quality In

It's not enough to deliver quickly of course. We also need to deliver safely. This means that we strive to deliver value to the customer that is free from defects. Anything which interferes with the customer getting value from the product is a defect.

Defects could come from mistakes in the coding process or they may come from misunderstanding the customer's needs. Both are defects which the team allowed to escape into production and cause the customer some inefficiency.

DevOps does not look to blame any individual for any escaped defect. The entire team is responsible and accountable for the quality of the product they develop. Rather we look at escaped defects as an opportunity to improve the entire process.

Some defects may be caught by automated unit, integration, contract, or end to end testing.

21

Some defects might be caught by peer or user testing. The team should review escaped defects, determine and track the causes. When patterns form there is opportunity to experiment and apply solutions to eliminate that source of defect.

DevOps practices talk of "shifting left" or shifting practices normally found later in the process to be done earlier in the process. For example if unit tests are normally only run during build, there may be some value in running them before commit instead.

The sooner defects are discovered, the easier and less costly they are to fix. Peer review that includes both a code review and a demonstration of the working code can be particularly helpful in discovering defects before they are committed, rather than after they are integrated into the mainline branch.

Invisible DevOps

As you can see from the above list of DevOps principles, none of these principles can be implemented solely by a separate DevOps team. DevOps is a culture, not a team. You can't have a "manager of culture" any more than you should have a "manager of DevOps" in your organization.

DevOps is a set of principles that are ingrained into empowered self-managing teams. These teams are hyper focused on delivering value to the customer in the simplest way possible. They are relentless in eliminating waste in the system and improving flow. They measure their progress with metrics that inform experimentation and decisions.

Throughout the rest of this book I will begin to describe the *Invisible DevOps* system. A system designed to create development teams that deliver value to the customer with a high flow rate.

The *Invisible DevOps* system is a framework consisting of several key components. Each of these components may be implemented differently in different organizations, but each component is vital to the operation of the system.

The *Invisible DevOps* system consists of:

- The DevOps Mindset
- DevOps Team Structure
- Continuous Improvement
- The Platform as a Product
- Embracing Cloud Paradigms
- DevOps Discipline Practices
- High Quality Delivery Pipeline

The first part of the book is concerned with the culture of DevOps: cultivating the DevOps mindset, organizing teams, and continuous improvement.

The second part deals with the practice of DevOps, or the practical day to day operational concerns which improve the DevOps capabilities of the teams: treating the platform as a product, embracing cloud paradigms, developer discipline practices, and the high quality delivery pipeline.

Chapter References

Graben, Mark. "*At Toyota: Mistakes are OK, as Long as We Learn; Culture and Psychological Safety*". Nov 17, 2022.

www.leanblog.org/2022/11/toyota-mistakes-o k-learn-culture-psychological-safety. Accessed Mar, 2022.

"Lean Thinking". modelthinkers.com/mental-model/lean-thinkin g. Accessed Mar, 2022.

Invisible DevOps

2 - DevOps Team Structure

Agile teams are composed of one product owner, one agile coach, and multiple developers. In the book *Team Topologies* by Michael Skelton and Manuel Pais, the authors describe these as "stream-aligned teams"

The teams are aligned to a value stream in the organization. This could be a single product, a single user experience, etc. They are long lived teams that work closely with the customer to deliver a continual stream of value: increment by increment.

This is the team structure we're probably all familiar with, however many organizations fall into a few traps

The Ops or DevOps Team

A long time ago, teams would be organized by function. There would be a development team, a database team, a quality team, an ops team, etc. In order for these teams to work together to build a product, there would be a series of slow and error prone handoffs from team to team.

Most organizations have started to do away with these silos, but the Ops team tends to be the last to go. This is the "Ops" that "DevOps" is primarily concerned with addressing.

As we learned last chapter, DevOps culture is one which empowers these stream-aligned teams and breaks down these functional silos.

The stream-aligned team needs to have all of the skills and capabilities they need to deliver the required value to the customer. The team needs to have front-end and back-end and testing and operations skills. The team must own and run the product they build.

If the stream-aligned team is building a product and hands it off to an Ops or DevOps team to run the product, then the stream-aligned team is missing out on valuable learning lessons and feedback they need to make the product better.

For example, if the containers used don't respond to SIGTERM well, it can be difficult to deploy new versions of the product. The Ops team would struggle with this every deployment, possibly having to manually babysit containers so they finish their work. They might request the change to the development team to make their work easier, but the development team doesn't feel the pain of operating their own software. This creates a lack of incentive for the team to fix the issue.

When the team feels the pain of operating their own software, they will prioritize improvements to the software to make it easier and safer to operate. The team doesn't want to wake up in the middle of the night to manually repair their product.

"Feeling the pain" results in a better product. A product that is resilient to errors, easy to deploy, and doesn't wake up its operators at night. Breaking down silos results in end to end ownership of the product. The definition of "done" for the team's work item becomes the only sane one: When the customer says it's done.

The Quality Team

Another remnant of the old ways is the quality assurance or quality engineering team being separate from the development teams. This team requires a detailed handoff from the development team to test the product and make sure it meets the requirements.

However, Agile teams tend to be light on documentation, favoring high bandwidth discussions between the developers and the product owners to share a vision of what the customer needs. The Quality Team tends to be absent from these discussions and doesn't share the vision when the shipped feature doesn't match the original work item description.

Furthermore, Agile development would assert that testing is the responsibility of the team producing the product, not an external team. Bob Martin takes this assertion further back in a 2007 JAOO panel discussion with Jim Coplien, stating that "it is irresponsible for a developer to ship a line of code that he has not executed in a unit test" and also that "it [is] infeasible for a software developer to consider himself professional if he does not practice [unit] test-driven development."

I would take this statement further than just saying there is value in writing tests before writing code. Developers need to write high value tests at the right level of abstraction (unit, integration, contract, regression, etc) to have a high confidence that their feature is working and is correct.

The majority of testing in a distributed system should be integration testing. Integration tests also cover much of what traditional unit tests cover, and any gaps in testing can be filled in with a smaller number of unit tests to avoid test duplication.

The reason for this is because in a distributed system, the features being developed are not in the units alone, but rather they are in the integration of units. Therefore our testing needs to focus more on the integrations than the units if we are to test the thing that our customers care about: features.

Now imagine that you have a Quality Engineering team that writes automated tests. You wish to be a professional developer in the eyes of your Uncle Bob, but how do you do this? How do you get Quality Engineering to write these high value tests before you write a line of production code?

The answer is that it's not possible--developers need to be responsible for producing high quality automated testing as they write production code. This just isn't possible with a siloed quality team, or even a cross functional team with a dedicated quality engineer. Neither of these team structures makes sense.

What does make sense is developers writing high value tests, at the right level of abstraction, that prove that their production code produces the value the customer desires.

There is a place for Quality Engineers in an organization like this, but it's not writing tests or testing products. The proper role for quality experts is to work as an enablement team. Such a team works to raise the automated testing quality and capability of the development teams through training or building testing frameworks.

The Small Agile Team

The agile team consists of a product owner, an agile coach, and developers. "Developers" is not used here in the traditional sense of software developer, but rather "the team members who are doing the work of the team." This could include many specialized skills the team needs, such as behavioral specialists for example, and not just software developers.

The team needs to have all of the skills required to develop the product and deliver the value to the customer. This allows the team to be a sort of communication island in the organization. These skills might be spread out among the team, or single individuals may have multiple skill sets. Ideally, the team will have multiple individuals who have each skill set the team needs.

Within the team there is a high degree of communication as the team works to solve problems and deliver value. Any time the team is required to communicate outside of their island, it slows the team down, introduces bottlenecks and blocked work items.

The product owner's role is to organize the customer's feedback and cast the vision for the product. They curate a list of product options in a backlog of potential work. The product owner needs to practice the agile principle of simplicity: maximizing the amount of work not done.

Therefore product options which are lower priority have the least amount of work invested in them and are least defined. Options which are highly likely to be worked on next have been defined to the point where the team can begin a discussion around how it could be implemented or broken down into smaller tasks.

The product owner is an equal member of the team. The team does not report to the product owner as this would create the wrong sort of team dynamic. The product owner is responsible for "what" value the customer needs next, while the developers are responsible for "how" they will deliver it.

The developers on the team are doing the work. They must receive and understand the product vision from the product owner. Not just the overall long term vision, but the vision for each iteration of value delivered to the customer.

If the team does not have the skills to develop, test, and deploy their solutions to the customer without having any slow handoffs to other teams, then the manager of the team must work to provide these skills either through training or hiring.

The Agile Coach is the only team member that might be part of multiple teams. The Agile Coach simply facilitates agile practices among the team. The coach is helping the team look at past iterations and metrics to improve the quality and flow of the team.

This agile team structure works best when the organization is small enough to have a single agile team working to deliver a single product. The authors point out in *Team Topologies* that due to Dunbar's number, a team like this can scale up to around 15 people before encountering communication problems, reduced trust, or lack of shared vision.

Conway's Law

> organizations design systems that mirror their own communication structure

Let's take a look at Conway's Law using the functional silos examples. Assume we have a development team, a database team, an ops team, and a quality team. What would Conway's Law predict about the structure of the product with these functional silos?

You might see that the infrastructure code is in a separate repository from the application code. This represents the ops team exerting their control over their repository and keeping it separate from the domain of the development team. However, separating infrastructure from application causes some difficulty in deployment.

Similarly there might be a separate repository for automated tests and a separate repository for data and schema migrations. Each of which combine to make a fragile and difficult release process.

Using the small agile team with one product example earlier, we would generally expect this team to produce something like a monolith or a distributed monolith type of system. The agile team is an island of communication and so is the monolith. All of the code, infrastructure, tests, and migrations are found in a single repository and versioned together. Releases become easier since all of the pieces necessary to perform the release are available in the single repository.

Many teams don't want to build monoliths, because we're told "monoliths are bad", and so they build a distributed system of services. However, due to Conway's Law, it's very difficult for a single team to build a distributed system of services without ending up with a distributed monolith.

A distributed monolith is one where the features are implemented across a lot of services and the services are so interdependent that it's difficult to release a single service in isolation. The team ends up coordinating release of the services so that they are all deployed together, just like a monolith would.

The problem is that the distributed monolith is harder to deploy than just a simple monolith. So the team ends up causing more work for themselves and pain when a simple monolith would deliver customer value better for a small single team. A single team facing the realization that they've built a distributed monolith might solve a lot of their headaches by refactoring into a simple monolith, or creating a mono-repo to ease deployment.

It is much easier to create a distributed system with well defined interfaces using multiple teams. Due to Conway's law, the separate teams will naturally create strong interfaces between the components to reduce the amount of communication necessary between the teams.

Multiple Teams and Conway's Law

Organizations don't stay single-team sized forever. Eventually organizations want to grow beyond the 15-person team size limit. How can we take into account good architecture design and Conway's Law to achieve this?

The answer is to design the agile architecture that best suits the product and then structure the organization to match the ideal architecture. This is obviously much harder in practice than in principle.

Multiple Teams, Multiple Products

One of the easiest ways to scale up is to put a second team on a second, independent stream of value. This might be a second product, or an isolated part of the product, such as an admin user experience.

This option isn't available for every organization since there may not be a second isolated value stream to work on. This also doesn't do anything to reduce the work and cognitive load of the original team.

It may be possible, such as the example of the admin interface, to split the product into truly isolated functions. This does reduce the cognitive load of the original team since they no longer need to be concerned about the split off functionality.

The new team needs to isolate and remove code from the repository of the first team so that they can have independent control of the new functional area of the product.

A micro-frontend strategy that allows each team to independently deploy parts of the application may be necessary. The simplest and most battle tested strategy is to have each team responsible for certain paths in the application, such as /user and /admin.

A Layer-7 load balancer or a reverse proxy can then route these paths to the different team's deployments. Each team has isolated development and deployment cycles but the user sees a cohesive experience.

Design systems and shared library components for common elements such as navigation will be required to ensure the user experience remains consistent between teams.

Complicated Sub-System Teams

A second team type talked about in *Team Topologies* is the complicated sub-system team. This is a team that handles a part of the system that requires most people on the team to have some kind of specialized knowledge.

For example, this might be a search engine, or a machine learning model, or an Identity Management component. Splitting off this complicated function from the original team will greatly reduce the cognitive load of the original team since the component requires a higher degree of skill and experience.

The complicated sub-system team needs to be handled with care to produce clear system boundaries and interfaces so that it does not require a high degree of communication between the two teams in order to integrate new features.

The complicated sub-system team should be a full agile team with a product owner, (possibly shared) agile coach, and a development team of up to 15 people. Generally this team will treat the stream-aligned team as their customer, but they may also have end-user facing components which require customer feedback. This team has an independent backlog of options and its own release cadence.

Some features may require both teams to participate in order to deliver a feature to the customer. In these cases, the work of the stream-aligned team is likely dependent on the complicated sub-system team. This work should remain in the stream-aligned team's backlog until it can be worked on without being blocked.

Once the dependency work is completed and deployed, the stream aligned team can begin the dependent work to deliver the feature.

Another way to think of this kind of shared work is that it originates from the product owner on the complicated sub-system. For example the team may want to implement a new way to perform search. They create the new feature in their API and then advocate for its use to the other teams. The other teams can then incorporate the new feature provided by the sub-system team without any dependencies or blocking. Communication is low between the teams if the API is well documented.

Platform Team

The platform team is like the complicated sub-system team. This type of team is designed to reduce the cognitive load of the stream-aligned teams.

An organization may want to hold off on creating a platform team until there are at least three stream-aligned or complicated sub-system teams that are independently deploying code.

The reason for this is similar to the "rule of three" method of refactoring, or "three strikes and you refactor". The rule of three teaches that the first time you build a feature, you just build it without considering or planning for any future possible abstractions. The second time you build a very similar thing, again, just build it without refactoring the first implementation--even if you need to copy and paste code. Once you have a third instance that is similar to the first, then you now have enough information and context to properly abstract and refactor your three cases into more manageable code.

The platform team is similar. The platform in this context is not your application architecture. Rather it is the way you think about and make use of your infrastructure and deployment pipeline. The platform is concerned with Cloud Infrastructure, Security, Logging, Monitoring, Alerting, Automating Recovery, Availability, Best Practices, Delivery Pipelines, etc.

All of these things require specialized knowledge and experience, so they increase the cognitive load of the stream-aligned teams. The platform team's role is to look at the ways the existing teams have solved these problems in order to abstract general solutions to take away this cognitive load.

This is much easier to do when there are already examples of deployments the teams are currently using to abstract into a generalized solution. Without this, the platform team runs the risk of creating a solution that requires the stream-aligned teams to significantly alter the way they work. This may lead to a low adoption of the platform team's work.

Care needs to be taken to ensure the platform team does not become the "ops" team. Individual teams still need to own and run their products themselves without handoffs. They still require the "ops" skillset in their team, but the use of easier self-service tools from the platform team should reduce the cognitive load.

I go into more detail about treating the Platform as a Product in Chapter 4.

Enablement Teams

Team Topologies talks about another team structure called an enablement team, but I won't go into too much detail about this team structure in this book.

The goal of the enablement team is to be a small team of experts in a particular field (e.g.

Security, Deployment, Testing, etc) which works closely with the stream-aligned teams on various short-lived projects.

The goal of these projects and engagements are to raise the capabilities of the stream-aligned teams, either through training or creating a framework that makes these areas of specialized work easier for the team to implement.

Ultimately this can reduce the cognitive load on the stream-aligned teams which will improve their quality and flow.

Multiple Teams and One Product

As a last resort, if none of the other options are available to the organization to improve flow, then consider having multiple stream-aligned teams working on the same product.

The reason this is a last resort is because this organization structure requires a high degree of communication between teams, and it blurs the ownership responsibility of the shared product. When multiple teams own something, then neither team really does.

Every deployment needs to be coordinated between the two teams which will slow down the flow of both teams.

This is a complicated team structure that should be avoided if possible. Instead favor team structures and ownership that have the most isolation between teams.

Teams and Invisible DevOps

The *Invisible DevOps* system can start small with one empowered agile team and one product. The team is the smallest unit of accountability. Success and failure are both shared by the team. Each component of the system must be owned by a single team.

As the organization grows, the main concern for *Invisible DevOps* is to reduce the cognitive load of the team while keeping a high level of communication separation between the teams so that each team can remain as independent as possible.

If there are complicated sub-systems, company growth can start there to split the team's responsibility and reduce the cognitive load.

If there are multiple products or clearly delineated sub-products, expand to multiple stream-aligned teams with isolated products and communication.

Once there are several stream aligned teams then invest in a platform team to abstract and standardize the infrastructure platform the teams have already been using.

Use enablement teams to spread knowledge of specific domains and to build frameworks to reduce team cognitive load around these disciplines.

Chapter References

Skelton, Mathew, and Manuel Pais. *Team Topologies*. E-book. IT Revolution Press, 2019.

Jim Coplien and Bob Martin Debate TDD. youtube.com/watch?v=KtHQGs3zFAM. Oct 23, 2012. Accessed April 1, 2023.

3 - Continuous Improvement

The third component of the *Invisible DevOps* system is to implement a culture of continuous improvement. This should primarily be done at the team level, in every team across the organization. Teams need to be empowered to run improvement experiments alongside delivering value to the customer.

This work does take some capacity away from the team, but the benefits outweigh the costs. Continuous Improvement can help the organization to reduce waste and rework. It should also be used to reduce the likelihood of litigation or security breaches. The team can become more engaged in their work knowing they are empowered to improve their process and flow. All of this will result in better customer retention and experience with the company.

In addition, all companies are looking for a competitive advantage. Continuous improvement is small changes over time, but these changes done consistently will result in a more agile, leaner company with a competitive advantage in the marketplace.

The lessons learned from continuous improvement can be shared between teams to raise the practice of the entire organization. Quality will improve and flow will ultimately increase in the long run.

What is Continuous Improvement?

Continuous improvement is a slow and steady framework for making incremental improvements to the business, rather than the product.

This is a measurable process using evidence to make decisions about whether the tested improvements are working or not. Each potential improvement is tested before being widely adopted.

Continuous improvement focuses on real problems or deficiencies in the business that can be measured and tracked over time.

This is also a lightweight agile process that is easy to adjust or abandon if proposed changes are not achieving the expected results.

What are we Improving?

The focus of continuous improvement is anything which represents a risk to the business that can be measured and improved.

The most visible area for improvement is cycle time and defect escape rate for teams. Cycle time measures how long it takes for a work item to be completed after it begins. This measures the elapsed real time from the moment the work item moves to "in progress" until when it has been moved to "done", or in the hands of the customer.

Defect escape rate is another common metric for improvement which measures the number of bugs which have been reported in production. Bugs in this case should be reported as both code defects and requirements defects. In either case, the customer was impacted with a product that did not fully meet their needs and requires rework.

Any form of waste can be reduced using continuous improvement as well. Waste could be anything from a team having to wait for another team, an underutilized resource or skill, an overutilized resource or skill, premature optimization, refactoring, or abstraction, low-value automated tests, etc.

Security or Regulation concerns can also be addressed in an incremental way to bring the business into compliance with a security framework.

We should not use any metrics which are tied to team performance reviews or bonuses. Some organizations try to measure story point velocity, lines of code written, or other velocity metrics. These types of metrics result in developers "gaming the system" to make the metrics look good, and should not be used in an organization.

How can we Improve?

There are many continuous improvement frameworks that could be adopted by the organization. One of the simplest ones to consider is the Plan-Do-Check-Act cycle.

The PDCA is a simple, agile framework for continuous improvement, and so it is an ideal choice for implementing *Invisible DevOps* as well. PDCA focuses on implementing solutions based on experiments and concrete evidence of results obtained from those experiments. *Kaizen* is another framework option that has been made popular by Toyota manufacturing.

During the *Plan* phase of PDCA, you identify a deficiency in the organization that you would like to focus on improving. With some investigation you identify a root cause and suggest potential solutions. You measure the current state and create a target for improvement.

Once this is done, you move into the *Do* phase of PDCA. You run a small scale experiment of one of your solutions in a way that will provide meaningful measurements to make a decision. While running the experiment, you must collect data that is analyzed in the next phase.

During the *Check* phase, you evaluate the results of your experiment. Did the proposed solution improve the situation any? Were there any issues or concerns that arose during the experiment that would prevent it from being deployed on a wider scale? Did we meet the measurement targets?

If the experiment was a success it is implemented on a wider scale across the team or organization in the *Act* phase of PDCA. This improved version of the deficiency becomes the new baseline for future improvements. If there was an improvement, but the target measurement was not yet met, then additional PDCA cycles can be run to further refine this solution. If the experiment was a failure, then other proposed solutions can be tried next.

Lastly, we need to be patient with the process and celebrate successes. Continuous improvement takes time and investment, but the payoffs are worth it. We need to allow the teams to run experiments, celebrate their successes, and encourage them to learn and continue if the experiments fail.

A culture of Improvement

In order for Agile or DevOps to be successful in the organization, there must be a culture of improvement throughout the organization. We should never be satisfied with the status quo and always looking to improve our tools, processes, and skills.

Every person in the organization needs to feel like they can make a difference and positive change in the organization. Teams must be empowered to improve their own processes rather than their process being dictated from above (which creates apathy in the team)

The organization must celebrate improvement successes and communicate the culture to everyone. The continuous improvement framework education should be made part of employee onboarding, showing examples of past experiments and outcomes.

One way to communicate successes is to use a catalog of Problem-Action-Result statements. These are succinct statements of what problems have been tackled (including the original metrics), what was done to improve the problem, and then end result metrics. This provides the company a running history of improvement that employees can look back on for inspiration to fuel future improvements.

Improvements generally should originate from the team that wants to improve themselves. There should be a sense of ownership in the process rather than something assigned to the team. Experiments will be more successful if the team feels empowered and accountable to improve.

Leadership's role is to provide the team the resources necessary to succeed.

Chapter References

What is the Plan-Do-Check-Act (PDCA) Cycle? asq.org/quality-resources/pdca-cycle. Accessed April, 2022.

Rule of three (computer programming). en.wikipedia.org/wiki/Rule_of_three_(computer _programming). Accessed Apr, 2022.

Part II
DevOps Practice

Invisible DevOps

4 - The Platform as a Product

In chapter 2, I talked briefly about platform teams and the platform. Treating your platform as a product is an important part of the *Invisible DevOps* system.

In the past, organizations would hire "DevOps engineers" and create a "DevOps team". The goal of these teams should have been to create the platform, or to be the platform team. However many organizations failed to realize this benefit. Their DevOps teams end up as another silo or a gate to delivery. It's never too late to restructure DevOps teams into what the platform team should be.

The need for a Platform

For many years, Puppet has been creating *The State of DevOps* report. They poll professionals from hundreds of organizations asking questions about how well their companies have implemented DevOps.

In 2023, after noticing a pattern surrounding the platform, they changed the format of their report to focus specifically on platform teams.

They had been noticing a significant gap between low and high performing DevOps organizations. What seemed to separate the middle performers from the high performers was the presence of a platform team, and treating the platform like a product.

The *Invisible DevOps* system recommends not forming a platform team until there are at least three stream-aligned or complicated sub-system teams already in the organization. This allows the "rule of three" to be applied to the work of refactoring and abstracting the platform.

What is the platform?

The platform is different from the application architecture. The platform is the method and systems used to create the infrastructure your application will run on and the delivery pipeline for your application.

If your application is run in the public cloud, the platform is the thin layer on top of this infrastructure-as-a-service that makes it easier and faster for the team to develop and deliver value to the customer.

Most tools your teams are using for the platform will be general purpose tools. The platform team will be able to create much easier to use special purpose tools that are built for your organization's specific needs.

The platform encapsulates industry and team best practices for deployment, security, compliance, logging, monitoring, etc. The goal of the platform is to make "the right way" be "the easy way" for the team to operate.

In larger organizations with a platform team, the platform is a first class product citizen. The platform team has its own product manager and Agile team delivering value to the other development teams.

The platform in these organizations becomes a self-service platform-as-a-service to the development teams. The platform team takes the deployment methods and best practices learned by the teams and incorporates them into the platform to help standardize learning across the organization.

The platform is not only the tools built internally, but may include many 3rd party services, such as github, datadog, and other SaaS services.

Benefits of Having a Good Platform

Every organization has a platform, whether or not they could point to it and explain it. Treating your platform as a product allows the organization to recognize its importance and iterate on improvement.

Generally the first and most important part of the platform is the delivery pipeline. I describe the delivery pipeline in more detail in Chapter 7. The goal of this pipeline is to deliver your increments of value to the customer as quickly and safely as possible. The quicker and safer this pipeline is, the more frequently you can deliver value to your customer and get feedback.

Security is another important aspect of the platform. The public cloud provides many security features, but they need to be used correctly to provide good security for the application. Production environments should be locked down to prevent any access from outside or inside the organization.

The platform needs to provide observability in such an environment for debugging. The platform can provide good logging and telemetry from the application as well as controlled means for inspecting production data and applying migrations. This allows the application security to remain strong in production.

Similarly the platform can help with other non-functional requirements such as legal compliance, performance, scalability, etc.

In many organizations where the platform isn't recognized, these requirements are generally achieved by writing some documentation to guide developers. These organizations rely on developers all having the skills and time required to implement such features.

Most development teams are under severe time pressure to deliver features to the customer and have trouble balancing these non-functional requirements. The organizations that treat the platform as a product understand the importance of developing these non-functional requirements as well as the functional ones.

The platform allows organizations to standardize security or scalability or compliance in a way that all new features developed automatically inherit these good practices. This allows teams to move faster in a safer way, while delivering a higher quality product to the customer.

Small Organization Platforms

When you're a smaller organization with only one or two development teams, you won't yet feel the need to create a platform team.

Development teams still need to start thinking about their platform as a product at this stage. It won't yet be a full fledged product with a separate product owner. However, the product owner needs to understand the importance of a platform for the team's application.

If the application has many services or components, think about the ways the deployments of these components can be standardized and streamlined. How can automated testing be incorporated into the delivery? How can you reduce or eliminate the need to access the production environment during debugging?

It takes some intentionality to make this work for a small team. The team needs to include some platform iterations along with product iterations to make improvements. Work on the product doesn't need to stop, rather the goal is to make continuous small improvements on the platform itself along with the product.

Some future thinking can be helpful here. The company will either grow or go out of business. Eventually there will be more teams and more developers. The work the team does on the platform is preparation for future growth.

The platform should include the development experience as well. How can you make it easy to onboard new developers? What can you do to make your development environments more like production? How can you make it easy to build and run automated tests in the development and test environments?

Each organization and product is going to have a different platform. While there are many common components to a platform, how these components are implemented will vary according to the preferences of the organization and teams.

Some standard platform components are described at the end of this chapter. Look around to other organizations who have implemented similar components and choose an implementation that fits your company's size, goals, and preference.

The Platform in Larger Organizations

When the organization grows beyond 3 or 4 teams, then it may be time to abstract the platform using a platform team.

At this point, your teams may be working independently on isolated products, and may have several different implementations of platform components. This works fine within the team, but developers moved between teams may experience difficulty in adjusting to new tools and processes.

Cost may be another factor in the desire to standardize on a set of tools across the organization. 3rd party services and tools don't always come cheap, and if each team has a different tool this can add up quickly.

The platform team has to start with the existing platforms that the development teams have already created and make small and frequent iterations to abstract these into a common platform.

It does no good for a platform team to develop a great platform in isolation, only to have no development team want to adopt the new platform. Care needs to be taken here, since the development teams will need to be involved in migrating to a standard platform. The standard platform has to provide a clear advantage to the team: saving them time or money.

Most likely the platform team will end up consolidating some components or leaving some options for the team. For example, you might decide to support both AWS Code Pipeline and CircleCI as pipeline tools because teams are heavily invested in both tools. The platform team would then build out common shared components for these two services to standardize how they are used.

Most likely the teams are also using one or more development frameworks such as Amplify, serverless.com, next.js, laravel, etc. These frameworks make developing easier in the development environment, but they also tend to provide deployment tools.

Rather than trying to standardize on one deployment method, these framework deployment tools should be supported by the platform because they generally make it easier and safer to deploy.

The number of environments is another common component that needs standardizing. This can be as simple as development, test, and production. It might also include environments for customer testing or other special purpose environments. The goal of the platform team is to be able to standardize where possible, but provide supported options where needed.

Development teams should also be free to implement solutions outside of the platform team as the need arises. However, these teams need to fully support their own application and custom platform if they choose not to make use of the platform team's solution.

In these cases, the platform product manager should seek to understand why the deviation was necessary and possibly plan for the platform to support these use cases in the future.

Standard Platform Components

Delivery Pipelines are used to orchestrate deployment of your application components to the environments in your runway, such as development, test, and production. Some example 3rd party pipelines are CircleCI, AWS CodePipeline, Github Actions, and laravel forge.

Deployment Tools are the means for moving code and configuration into an environment. This might be a general purpose tool such as AWS CodeDeploy or a framework specific tool such as serverless.com or laravel forge.

Migration Tools are tools which deal with the data layer. They include the ability to make changes to the schema as well as the data. These tools should be used to make any changes to production data rather than manual queries in production. The tools allow for peer review and provide an audit trail since they are generally committed alongside the application in the same repository. Some examples include alembic, laravel migrate, and liquibase.

Infrastructure as Code are infrastructure definitions that are committed alongside the application code in order to describe the infrastructure the application depends on. When the application is released, the infrastructure can be updated as required. Some examples are AWS Cloud Formation, AWS CDK, Terraform, and Azure Resource Manager.

Log Aggregation is a process for collecting all the application and system logs from an environment into a central location. This helps to prevent log tampering if the system is compromised as well as to facilitate debugging of remote systems without requiring terminal access. Some examples are AWS CloudWatch Logs, S3, Datadog, and Splunk.

Debugging tools can be part of the platform which include the ability to gain visibility into a production environment without reducing the security of the environment. Log aggregation is a big part of this, but also the ability to query read-only data from the system, inspect processes, etc. This might also include some form or zero-trust VPN to allow the team into the environment on a temporary basis.

Development Environment is an important part of the platform that makes it easy for developers to run a local version of the application for development and debugging. This might be a hybrid cloud-local environment as well to make use of managed cloud services while developing application code. Some frameworks like sst.dev include cloud-local development environments that simplify developing against cloud managed services. Other tools such as local stack attempt to emulate the cloud components in a fully local environment. The right tool for the team is going to depend on the language, frameworks, and cloud managed services being used.

Audit Logging is a process for shipping sensitive audit logs to a central write-only log location which can be used as part of a security and intrusion detection system. Some examples include AWS CloudTrail, or Splunk.

Monitoring is a means of collecting telemetry from the application so that its health can be inspected. This should include meaningful application insights such as the number of transactions. It should also capture error metrics such as failed 3rd part service calls, or application error rates. Some examples include AWS CloudWatch, Datadog, and Splunk.

Alerting is a means of being notified when a monitor falls outside of the normal bounds. Alerting should only be used for things that are urgently actionable by someone on the team. Too many alerts causes alert fatigue and reduced response time and team flow. The goal for all alerts is that they can be automatically handled by the application to recover state.

Guardrails are a type of security that prevent accidental or unwanted infrastructure or practices. They also prevent bad actors from doing certain things if they manage to get into the system. This could be anything from only allowing certain regions to be used, disallowing public IPs on instances, avoiding defaults for memory or cpu, or preventing infrastructure to be created without encryption at rest. Some examples include AWS Service Control Policies, AWS Config, or terraform sentinel.

Cost Management is a process for optimizing costs, assigning costs to teams, and reporting on cost usage. It might include alerts or limits on spending. Some examples include AWS cost management and billing alarms, CloudZero, and CloudCheckr.

Shared Infrastructure which is used by multiple teams might also be considered part of the platform. This might include shared busses, or shared physical cache or database servers which keep logical separation of services.

Best Practices are ways to make "the easy way" be "the right way". Some examples might be infrastructure patterns for deploying static websites using CloudFront and S3 in a secure way, or ensuring proper CORS headers are in place on API backing services. For example, Amazon CDK provides a construct library that allows patterns of infrastructure to have best practices for the organization baked into reusable infrastructure code.

Chapter References

2023 State of Platform Engineering Report. puppet.com/resources/state-of-platform-engineering. Feb 2023.

Rule of three (computer programming). en.wikipedia.org/wiki/Rule_of_three_(computer _programming). Accessed Apr 3, 2022.

Invisible DevOps

5 - Embracing Cloud Paradigms

Embracing cloud paradigms is another component of the *Invisible DevOps* system. In this chapter I'm going to give examples using AWS services specifically since I'm most familiar with the AWS public cloud. These principles can be used with any cloud that the team is using.

The Free Tier

Many cloud providers offer a free tier of services that small organizations or small applications can make use of. Traditional server applications can be more expensive to run in the cloud than in a datacenter, but there are ways of building applications in the cloud that are much cheaper.

I have hosted several applications in the cloud that cost no more than $0.50 per month. This cost was for the domain hosting in Route 53, while the application cost was free. This provides a great opportunity for small companies to start small and test the feasibility of their application in the market. As usage grows, the hosting costs will grow linearly making this a great option for new products.

An application like this consists of a front-end application hosted on S3 and CloudFront. This might be a SPA static HTML application or pre-compiled application without a server-side component.

The API component can be built with API Gateway and Lambda. Both of these services provide fairly generous free tiers.

Data storage using DynamoDB, a key-value cloud storage can be done within the free tier for applications with small read/write throughput.

A great number of applications can be built this way and hosted cheaply in the cloud. This provides a great opportunity for startups to manage their costs before they have paying customers.

Managed Services

One of the greatest advantages of the public cloud providers are the managed services they provide. Running a production ACID compliant database used to require a DBA with the skill to correctly tune the database, manage replication and backups, and monitor the database 24x7. In the cloud, databases can be defined with a few lines of infrastructure code and the cloud provider does all the heavy lifting of managing the database, replication, and backups.

This means that organizations taking advantage of these managed services no longer need to hire expensive experts to handle the cognitive load. Teams can move faster and experiment with complicated database, search, queue, bus, and pubsub services without becoming experts in server management, tuning, backups, and monitoring.

Using the *Invisible DevOps* system, organizations should make use of managed cloud services wherever possible to reduce the complexity of their application and platform.

These services also virtually eliminate the need for managing security patching as this function is generally managed by the service automatically.

Here are a sampling of AWS Managed Services that reduce cognitive load on the teams:

Relational Database Service (RDS) is a managed MySQL, Postgres, Oracle, or MSSQL relational database service. The standard RDS service runs these services on physical hardware that is well tuned to run databases in the cloud. The Aurora service is a custom Amazon service that separates the compute from storage in the database allowing them to scale independently to provide resilience and multi-region write capability.

ElastiCache is a managed Memcached or Redis cache. This service provides high availability without the need for running your own cache servers.

Elastic Beanstalk is a managed deployment service that can deploy server-side code such as PHP, python, node, java, docker, and other languages. This service automatically manages scaling of services in response to load metrics, and safely deploying migrations and code with zero-downtime deployments.

Elastic Container and Kubernetes Services are two different services (ECS and EKS) which manage container orchestration. These can be used to define services which can autoscale in response to load or run one-off container tasks in response to an event or schedule.

EventBridge, SNS, and SQS are bus, pubsub, and queue services that facilitate communication between application components.

Polly, Lex, Rekognition, Textract, and Transcribe are a few of the many AI powered managed services that AWS provides for various special purpose functions.

Lambda is a function-as-a-service that allows you to run code without managing servers. Lambda functions can be used with API gateway to create a fully serverless API with no servers to manage or patch.

Cloud Scalability

Another advantage of the cloud is its scalability. There is an incredible amount of extra capacity in the cloud that can be used to rapidly scale your application in response to increased traffic. Depending on the managed service used, this scaling response could be as short as a few seconds.

Putting in place managed autoscaling as part of the application platform will allow your team to respond automatically to customer growth without impacting team flow. Depending on your application's usage patterns this could also save you significant costs during slow traffic periods.

A service like AWS Batch can be used to automatically scale up batch processing in response to the number of incoming tasks.

If the application's traffic patterns are highly variable, then the application platform should include some form of auto scaling options to grow resources during high peak times and shrink resources during lower usage.

High Availability

Not all applications require extremely high levels of availability such as 99.999%. However the cloud's managed services and datacenter distributions makes it much easier to achieve availability as high as 99.95% fairly easily in a single region.

The cloud managed services will provide a means for running the service from multiple availability zones (physical data centers). Your application should be deployed into at least two availability zones as well.

With two availability zones used, AWS is designed to provide 99.99% availability for most services. The more services your application uses, the more your theoretical availability goes down.

For example, using API Gateway (99.99%) and ECS containers (99.99%) and Aurora database (99.99%) together results in a combined theoretical max SLA of .9999 * .9999 * .9999 = 99.97% providing that at least two availability zones are used for each service.

Much higher availability can be achieved by expanding into multiple regions, such as us-east and us-west. However, this requires the use of data storage services that can handle multi-region writes with low latency. Most applications don't actually need this level of availability and a single region, multiple availability zone strategy is often enough.

The application platform should enforce multi-availability zone deployments for all application code and managed services used in production. This default deployment pattern should be made easy for the team to accomplish.

Cloud Security

The cloud has a shared responsibility model for security. The cloud provider is responsible for securing the cloud itself, from the physical security of the datacenters to the logical security separating each customer. The cloud customer is responsible for the security of the applications they run in the cloud.

The more managed services used, the more security becomes the responsibility of the cloud provider, providing you have guardrails in place to provision those resources securely.

Take advantage of the encryption options these managed services provide. Create customer managed encryption keys for the application and encrypt all data at rest and in transit.

Store application secrets in a managed secrets provider that can pass those secrets securely to your application without exposing them to read-only users of the cloud console.

If you look at many of the breaches that were reported by SaaS companies, many of them took advantage of employee accounts. Hackers are targeting developer tools such as IDE plugins, or dependency hijacking to get into developer environments.

Locking employees out of production prevents such malicious activity by not giving developers access in the first place to be hijacked. Multi-Factor authentication doesn't prevent this type of attack which is able to grab the session credentials from the environment of IDEs or Pipeline orchestration tools.

Read-only accounts should be provisioned to employees who require access to production, and write access should be limited only to automation roles that apply infrastructure as code in the delivery pipeline. In rare cases, write access to production should be provisioned temporarily and this access audited in a log for review by the security team.

This protection is not because we don't trust our employees, but rather this is a very popular attack vector by malicious entities. This vector has been exploited in many of the publicly announced breaches, and the platform needs to help the company stay safe.

It is also a recommended practice to deploy applications into their own accounts in the cloud to maintain separation. Cloud accounts provide cost boundaries and security boundaries. Having a different account for each workload or product allows you to easily assign costs to the workload, as well as assign proper roles and permissions to the team.

Cost and Performance Optimization

Many cloud providers have tools to help optimize and balance cost and performance. These tools can track memory and cpu resource utilization and provide a report of over or under utilized resources.

For compute resources with strict memory and cpu limits such as containers and lambda functions, this sort of reporting is vital to keep track of to avoid hitting these limits.

The application platform needs to collect this data from the cloud provider and report to the teams when they need to adjust their infrastructure code to optimize memory and cpu settings for performance and cost.

On demand usage is generally higher cost than purchasing payment plans from cloud providers. Some payment methods like spot instances or fargate spot could save up to 80% of the cost over on-demand pricing. The platform should incorporate the tools provided by the cloud provider to point out these potential savings to the team.

Invisible DevOps in the Cloud

The application platform should function to help development teams to make the best use of the cloud. As much as possible, best practices need to be provided for free by the platform, so that the right way is the easy way.

Each separate product should have its own cloud account to separate costs and create security boundaries. Infrastructure code should be run through platform guardrails to ensure security practices like encryption and isolation.

Applications should be deployed in a highly available configuration by default. The development teams should have the option to add auto scaling, or multi-region deployments if it makes sense for the applications being deployed.

Provide cost and performance monitoring so that the teams can keep track of capacity.

Wherever possible, make use of managed services to reduce the cognitive and maintenance load of the teams.

Invisible DevOps

6 - DevOps Discipline Practices

Adam Wiggins, founder of the Heroku platform-as-a-service, published his observations on the twelve factor app around 2011. The twelve factor app is a blueprint for designing apps that will run well in a cloud environment, specifically the Heroku environment.

As it turns out, these twelve factors play a significant role in DevOps since they create an application that is much easier to deploy and manage. The full description of the twelve factor app can be found on the 12factor.net website, and I won't be repeating its contents here.

However, I would like to expand on the twelve factors as it relates specifically to DevOps and what I'm calling developer discipline practices. Some of these items are harder than others to implement well and consistently, but the more intentional and diligent we are at conforming to these development practices, the easier it will be to design, develop, build, release, and run our products.

I - Codebase

The twelve factor app has one codebase tracked in revision control, with many deploys. There should be one code repository for each deployable unit. If multiple components of a system need to be deployed together, such as in a distributed monolith, then all of the components should be co-located in the same repository. This is sometimes called a "mono-repo" and allows you to version and deploy tightly coupled components together.

The entrypoint into the delivery pipeline should be triggered by pushing to the mainline branch of the repository. Github, Gitlab, AWS CodeCommit, and BitBucket are all examples of repository services to host your codebase.

In addition to the application code, there are a few more things that should be co-located in the repository: tests, migrations, infrastructure, and dependency configuration.

The repository needs to contain all of the automated tests that are run against the repository. This allows the tests to be versioned with the application code and available to the delivery pipeline to be run when triggered.

Any schema or data migrations that the code requires should also be part of the application repository. This allows the delivery pipeline to run these migrations in each environment before deploying the application code.

Additionally, infrastructure code is also co-located with the repository. This represents infrastructure dependencies that your application requires to run, such as databases, queues, encryption keys, etc.

Some application dependency configuration will also be found here, such as configuration that relates to the 3rd party libraries the application uses, or the injection of infrastructure code dependencies. For example, the Infrastructure code might create a queue or database and pass the endpoint URL of this backing service to the application during deployment to an environment.

There should never be any sensitive data or secrets committed to a code repository. You should always assume that malicious actors will be able to access your codebase through malware or dependency supply chain attacks.

II - Dependencies

The twelve factor app explicitly declares and isolates dependencies. In the original twelve factor app, this goal was to not assume that any operating system or language dependencies would be already installed on the target machine the code would run on.

These dependencies would instead be declared using the package manager software that ships with the language (npm, pip, etc.). For example, for node projects, the package-lock.json file is a means for explicitly declaring application dependencies.

The application should rely on a build process that bundles the code together with its dependencies and configuration before deploying to an environment. Nothing should be assumed about the environment the code will run on other than assuming it will be a vanilla operating system.

I would like us to take this concept a little farther when it comes to DevOps. In addition to language dependencies or packages, the application needs to declare some other dependencies as well.

Infrastructure is one of those dependencies. Applications must run on some kind of hardware environment. Most applications require a data store. Applications might require additional infrastructure like cache, load balancer, DNS records, queues, busses, etc.

The application needs to be able to explicitly declare these dependencies as well. This is what's known as Infrastructure as Code (IaC). This infrastructure code needs to be committed along with the application code in the same repository. This allows the delivery pipeline to apply changes to the infrastructure into the environment before migrations and code are deployed.

Some development frameworks, such as serverless.com or sst.dev have infrastructure code built into the framework. If you aren't using a framework like this, you might need a special purpose IaC framework such as AWS Cloud Development Kit (CDK) or Terraform.

The goal of this level of dependency management should be to have the ability to start with an empty cloud account, deploy the infrastructure code, deploy the migrations, and deploy the application code to get a complete working application environment.

If you are deploying with containers or as Lambda functions, then memory and CPU are also dependencies that need to be declared. Your application needs to specify a memory and CPU setting that balances performance requirements and cost.

If this is required by your application, be sure to have a means for monitoring memory and CPU usage to ensure that these limits are not being reached by the application. Provide enough headroom that you don't have to urgently respond to these alarms.

III - Config

Configuration that changes between deployments or environments belongs in environment variables passed to the application at runtime. For example, the infrastructure code will generate endpoint URLs for databases and queues. These URLs need to be configured in the application. The application can expect to find these URLs in environment variables at runtime. The infrastructure code can be configured to pass these variables to the application automatically so that they don't have to be manually configured per environment.

In a local development environment, developers might create the cloud resources in a sandbox account and set their local environment to point to the cloud sandbox resources through a .env file.

Front-end code can also be compiled with environment variables at build time and deployed as static assets. No secrets should be passed to front-end code, however as these are viewable by the public.

Some types of configurations do not change with each deployment. Some examples of this include an API framework's routing paths, a dependency injection configuration file, etc. Any configuration that is not secret and does not change per environment should be committed in the repository along with the application code. This helps to simplify the environment configuration and reduce manual configuration.

Infrastructure configuration is like this as well. An application might need only 1 replica in the test environment, but needs 4-10 replicas of the application to handle customer traffic in production. This kind of environment configuration can be committed in the infrastructure code.

Secret values need to be treated differently. Secret values include database passwords, private keys, 3rd party API keys or tokens, IAM credentials, etc.

These values should never be committed into a repository and may require some manual configuration in each environment. With each type of deployment, the cloud provider should provide a mechanism for passing secret configuration to an application at runtime.

For example, Amazon ECS is a container service. The managed service provides an integration with AWS Secrets Manager to be able to decrypt the secrets and pass them automatically into environment variables that the application can read at runtime.

AWS Lambda, by contrast, doesn't have as tight of an integration and requires the secret location to be passed in the environment. The application then needs to call Secrets Manager with the secret location to retrieve the secret values during function initialization.

Some secret values, such as database credentials, can be automatically generated by the infrastructure code, stored in a secret, and passed securely to the application in a completely automated way without a person having to ever see the secret value.

Others like 3rd party access tokens will have to be manually configured in a secret in the environment so that the application can use it.

IV - Backing Services

In the twelve factor app model, applications are supposed to treat all backing services as attached resources. The reason for this is so that the application never assumes that a required service is always going to be on the same server the application is deployed to.

This makes sense from a scalability perspective. If the application is a web server that has a database, you want to be able to scale the number of web servers independently from the number of databases. Treating as a backing service means to expect all services to be found by a URI, typically an address and port.

These addresses are environment specific configuration and will be found in the application's environment variables. This allows for development and test environments to co-locate services on a single machine for cost savings, while placing them in pools behind load balancers in a production environment. The application code remains the same, only configuration changes.

Error handling with backing services

One important discipline practice around backing services is error handling. Applications need to be fault tolerant in the cloud. Applications can't even rely on the local filesystem to be available when it performs a write, and any remote services are much less reliable.

DevOps culture is one where we focus on the customer experience. Backing services are unreliable by their nature, and so they need to be handled with care to ensure a good user experience.

For example, if a 3rd party service is used to write data and that service returns a 5xx error, what should the application do?

First, any 5xx or 429 error is retryable, so the application should be configured to retry a number of times with exponential backoff. If the write still fails to the backing service, then some kind of fallback is required to preserve the end user experience.

One fallback method is eventual consistency. The request might be queued for later processing, and the user presented a message such as "Sorry, it's taking longer than expected to process your request. We'll keep trying and notify you when it's done"

Another fallback method is to provide a default value instead of a user personalized value. The user might be presented with a "Sorry, we don't have any good recommendations right now, here's some popular articles you might like instead"

It might be possible to provide a cached value from a previous call, even if that cache is stale. This still provides the user with data, even though it might not be the latest data. Progressive Web Apps function in this sort of "cache-first" way of presenting data to the user.

For services that are deep in the call chain, they might just return something like a 424 error themselves (not a 5xx to prevent the upstream service from retrying the request). This allows the error to be handled at a higher context that might be able to generate a better user experience.

Be sure to include small connection timeouts on all backing service calls. Connection timeouts for services within your own network can be as short as 2 seconds, while timeouts for connections across the internet might need to be 5 to 10 seconds.

Secondarily, after the connection is successful, use a second response timeout while waiting for processing. This might be as high as 30 seconds.

If either timeout is reached, assume the call has failed and use normal retry and fallback logic.

Backward compatibility

An extremely important discipline related to backing services is backward compatibility. Backward compatibility relates to the public interface contract of a backing service.

When an application declares its dependency on a backing service, it's really declaring a dependency on a major version of an interface contract that some concrete backing service will provide.

That backing service might be a MySQL database running on an EC2 instance, for example. The dependency is on the MySQL protocol of some major version, such as v8. That MySQL server could be swapped for an Aurora RDS server instead. Aurora is not MySQL, but it provides a MySQL compatible interface. The application doesn't care what the concrete implementation is, so long as it honors the MySQL v8 interface contract.

Your application might be a backing service for another application as well. This is quite common in a microservices architecture where there are many services that work together to produce features and value for the user. In order to maintain the ability for services to be deployed independent of other services, the development discipline of backward compatibility is critical.

Within a major version, no compatibility breaks are allowed. The easiest way to accomplish this is to only allow additive changes to your public interface. Creating new methods doesn't break old methods. You can add a new optional property to a method call that defaults to a reasonable value. Any change which doesn't require a change in the way a calling service functions is okay.

There is another reason that backward compatibility is critical for a DevOps environment, and that is deployment. During a typical software deployment, two versions of your application code will be running at the same time. The scheduler might deploy the new version of your code and wait for it to report healthy before it removes the old version of the code. This is required for a zero-downtime deployment.

Imagine that your application code relies on a database backing service with a particular schema. During a deployment, you will run the schema migrations first, before updating the code. While the code is updating, both the old and new versions of the code will be running against the same updated database schema.

If the schema changes made are not backward compatible, such as dropping or renaming a column, the old code will produce errors during the deployment, resulting in a bad user experience. Worse yet, data might become corrupted if the old code writes to the database after a migration changes the way data is stored. This will result in a manual data cleanup effort.

The same is true for any dependency, such as one service calling another. If the dependency service changes its interface in an incompatible way, the calling service will fail and produce errors for the user.

Backwards compatibility is a critical component to safe deployments.

Idempotency

Idempotency is also an important discipline in a distributed system. When your service is a backing service, it must be idempotent. Idempotency is the ability of a service to respond correctly to repeated calls with the same data.

Repeated calls occur because the calling services need to handle error conditions and retry calls. Sometimes successful or partially successful calls are retried. A network failure preventing the called service from responding may have completed the work but failed to respond. The calling service would then retry a completed call.

This is also an issue with queues, buses, or pubsub architectures. Most of these services offer an at-least-once guarantee of delivery, and not exactly-once. Your application might receive a message from one of these services multiple times and needs to handle this case appropriately.

Another possibility is that your application hit a memory limit and was terminated in the middle of processing a work item. The work item would then be resubmitted to another worker. The second worker would need to be able to apply the work item regardless of the state left by the first worker.

Another possibility is that the calling service has a short timeout for the response (or a user is impatient and clicked again). If it hits this timeout and retries the call it is possible the second call is running concurrently with the first call still being processed.

Your application might be able to handle a lot of these concerns by using database transactions that are rolled back on error. It might also need a method to detect duplicate calls, such as using a caller-generated unique ID for each request. Using such an ID might allow the application to return the original response to a duplicate request without performing any processing, for example.

Idempotency is not easy to accomplish, but it is a developer discipline that will improve your deployment safety, and save you a lot of headaches and data cleanup if done right.

Idempotency rules for calling services:

- Debounce requests to the called service
- Retry on 429 and 5xx errors
- Retry with exponential backoff
- Stop retrying on other 4xx errors
- Send a unique ID for request and retries

- Have a short connect timeout
- Have a longer response timeout
- Implement fallback logic on failures
- Present the user the best possible degraded user experience on failures

Idempotency rules for called services:

- Assume all requests are duplicates
- Check if the work is already done
- Check if ALL the work is already done
- Complete any outstanding work
- Reply with 5xx to request caller to retry
- Reply with 429 if you're overloaded
- Reply with 424 to stop caller from retrying if there are downstream errors
- Return duplicate response for same unique request ID

V - Build, Release, Run

The twelve factor app calls for strictly separated build, release, and run stages. Along the deployment pipeline, there should ideally be one build, and many releases. a build is the compile step required to create the code asset. The deployment step is the act of combining this code asset with environment configuration. Code is then run in an environment with this environment specific configuration available in its environment variables.

The goal of a single build and many deploys is not possible with some deployment tools. For example, front-end static HTML needs to be compiled with the environment variables in it. This necessitates a separate build for each environment. Other development tools such as serverless.com work in a similar way and have to be built for each environment. This is an acceptable deviation from the twelve factor app model, because it is using tried and tested deployment tools to do this work, and the only changes to the compiled asset will be the environment specific configuration changes.

The build step will typically include unit testing to validate the build. I discuss automated testing in more detail in Chapter 7. The goal of this testing is to balance the value of these tests against the speed of the build. The slower the build and test process, the longer it will take for a code change to go through the delivery pipeline.

While the build stage may be relatively long, such as 20 minutes, the run stage needs to be very fast. Deploying compiled assets should be done as quickly as possible to minimize the amount of time between starting the new version and the orchestrator being able to validate the health check of the new version.

If the new version needs to be rolled back, having a quick application startup will get the environment back to full capacity quickly.

Chapter 7 includes more detail on how to build a delivery pipeline that has this build-release-run separation in it. A more complete discussion on developer discipline around automated testing is discussed there as well.

VI - Process

The twelve factor app executes as one or more stateless processes. The application code must not assume that any data cached locally will be available on subsequent runs. This includes the local file system or in-memory caches. Any persistent state data must be stored in a persistent (permanent or temporary) backing store, such as a database, memcached, or redis.

For a web application, it can be helpful to use signed or encrypted JWT token passed in the Cookie or Authorization headers to maintain session state. A minimal amount of data can be stored in the token (less than 2k is recommended) to identify the user. The signature on the token along with the expiration date can be used to validate the user's authenticated state without having to validate this with the persistent backing store.

Standardizing Deployment Types

It can be helpful for development teams to standardize on how they will deploy applications using the process model. Almost any application could be deployed using a combination of containers and lambda functions, for example.

Thinking about deployment at the container or function level like this allows development teams to use any number of languages they require while standardizing the way these applications are deployed and managed.

This allows the team to create a standardized pipeline that works the same way across a wide variety of languages and applications. This is an example of treating the platform as a product and abstracting deployment methods.

VII - Port Binding

The only way to communicate between applications should be through well defined ports and protocols. This allows for the composition of services, where one service can become a backing service for another by configuring the URL to the backing service in the environment.

Exposing services via port binding is the natural way that containers are deployed. Lambda functions on the other hand are exposed through API calls (https ports) instead and can be integrated directly with many AWS services such as Event Bridge, SQS, and SNS.

Access services through public interface only

The port binding requirement can also be thought of as the public interface for the application or service. The public port exposed should be the only part of the service that is directly accessed. Using the SOLID principles, no internal part of a service, such as a data store, should be directly accessed by another service.

VIII - Concurrency

Applications should scale out via the process model. This is where the twelve factor app really shines as a solution for scalability. Rather than scaling vertically adding more CPU or RAM to a single monolithic process, multiple smaller stateless processes are used. Because the processes are stateless, they can be added quickly as traffic increases using auto scaling, to meet the demand required.

By breaking down your larger application into separate deployable twelve factor applications, different components can be scaled independently from each other.

A process running in Docker that is reading from a queue may scale up in response to a high volume of requests in the queue. A web process might scale up in response to increased CPU or memory pressure, request volume, or for peak hours.

It is important that scaling activities are automated, so that developers can focus on writing new application features rather than responding to production application load.

Deployment by Availability Requirements

An important development discipline is to take availability requirements into account when deploying services. A cloud provider will provide some SLA guarantees if the application is properly deployed.

From a user experience perspective, a user probably has an expectation for something like 99.999% availability. This is equivalent to an experience like this: "The app is always available when I go to use it, but once a day, the application takes more than 1 second to load."

In practice, it can be quite difficult and costly to guarantee five-nines availability. It requires deploying the application into multiple regions and multiple availability zones in those regions. Each region would have to have an actively running capacity that could handle 100% of the user traffic alone, so the cost of the application is doubled.

An application running in a single region using multiple availability zones in the cloud can quite easily achieve a 99.95% availability, which allows for about 45 seconds of downtime per day on average.

Less critical services or components could be deployed with reduced redundancy to achieve a lower availability around 99.5% to 99.9% which allows for around 2 days of downtime per year.

Developers should be aware of their availability requirements for services and deploy critical services to meet high availability requirements and deploy less critical services using reduced redundancy to save costs.

Applications need enough concurrency to meet user demand as well as enough redundancy to handle service outages. If the application requires 2 replicas to handle user load, then it might need 2 replicas in each of 2 availability zones, or 4 total replicas, to meet availability and capacity requirements. If availability is not as important, you might deploy 1 replica in each of 2 availability zones, and then rely on the scheduler to launch another replica if one zone becomes unavailable to meet capacity needs. The application will be under provisioned for a period of time in this case which might create a poor user experience.

IX - Disposability

In a cloud environment, applications have to expect that their compute resource may become unavailable at any time. To mitigate this fact, applications need to maximize robustness with fast startup and graceful shutdown.

Applications need to be able to start fast so that they can respond quickly to scaling events when more capacity is required. Fast startups also make configuration changes quicker, which is required to respond to certain failures in backing services, such as a database restore or a region failover.

Applications must also be designed to crash unexpectedly in the cloud. An application running in any environment might experience hardware failures. However, there are some additional factors in the cloud environment that can cause applications to stop unexpectedly.

For example, a lambda function has an explicit time and memory limit. Exceeding the time limit or memory limit will cause the function to end suddenly. Docker containers running in fargate have similar memory limits, but can run for longer periods of time. When using spot instances to save money on compute resources, those instances can be reclaimed with a 2 minute warning that will issue SIGTERM to any containers running in ECS before killing the containers with SIGKILL. When docker containers running in ECS are scaled in, they will similarly be signaled by a SIGTERM followed by a SIGKILL 30 seconds later.

In order to deploy applications in such a hostile environment, your applications need to be able to crash gracefully and recover quickly. For any web server type of application, this is generally not a problem if the web server application is stateless. Containers can be drained from the load balancer and killed without having any impact on user interaction, so long as all web requests are shorter than 30 seconds. Processes that take longer than 30 seconds need to be run as background processes out of a queue.

For longer running background processes that are processing a queue, the jobs must be able to either checkpoint and restart with transactions, or be idempotent so that multiple runs of the job will produce the same results. The job framework used might help with this process by automatically re-submitting jobs to the queue if the worker exits with an error.

Lambda functions can be thought of as running once and disposed of, since the function container might not be reused on the next call.

For docker-based deployments, the required developer discipline is that all container instances must listen for the SIGTERM signal on process pid 1. Upon receiving this signal, they need to shut down gracefully within 30 seconds.

Any long running processes which receive the SIGTERM signal, should checkpoint their work and shut down gracefully, allowing a different process to continue the work from the checkpoint. Alternatively they might have time to rollback the transaction so it can be started again.

This SIGTERM process is also used by the Infrastructure to warn the container instances that the physical hardware backing the containers is being shut down. Because of this, any containers which do not respond gracefully to SIGTERM will become abruptly terminated at some point and could leave data in a corrupted state.

This SIGTERM signal is also used by container orchestrators during deployment. Responding gracefully to this signal is critical to delivery pipeline safety.

X - Development/Production Parity

The goal of the delivery pipeline should be to keep development, test, and production environments as similar as possible. This allows for testing that is performed in the lower environments to give a high level of confidence that the application will perform correctly in production.

Containers and Lambda functions are often used by developers because they provide an environment for the application that is consistent from development to production.

Backing services, such as databases, should be of the same type that is used in production environments rather than using lightweight alternatives. For example, try not to use sqlite in development but postgres in production.

If possible, the use of cloud services should not be simulated through tools like local stack. Instead use the actual cloud services in a development environment. This ensures that the behavior of these cloud services in development will be identical to the behavior of those services when run in production, especially as it relates to application roles and permissions.

Where possible, the use of developer framework tools can help a lot here. For example, sst.dev allows for infrastructure code to be deployed in a sandbox using API Gateway, while the API's lambda function invocations are routed to a local development environment where breakpoints and other IDE tools can be used to facilitate development and debugging.

XI - Logs

Good logging is another important developer discipline. The twelve factor app requires that logs are treated as event streams. Using lambda or containers, logs are treated as event streams by default by having the application simply log to stdout and stderr.

Applications should not be trying to manage log files on a file system. If this sort of logging is required, an application like rotatelogs can be used to read the stdout logs and write to rotated logs to prevent filling the disk.

However these logs are more useful when centralized in a log store such as cloudwatch logs or datadog. All logs should be logged in a structured format like JSON rather than plaintext messages like "INFO: transaction finished". JSON logging allows the log aggregation tools to provide better searching and filtering of log messages when trying to debug application problems in an environment.

When in a development environment, these JSON logs can be pretty formatted in stdout so they are easier to read. In other environments they should not have any newline characters, one log entry per line.

Logging needs to have a high signal to noise ratio to be useful. Avoid any sort of debug logging outside of development. When logging web requests from the application, use a single log entry which captures the full request and response including headers, but excluding any sensitive data like passwords or authorization tokens. Avoid any logging mid-request. The logging should have enough information to trace the code from start to finish given the request and response data. This data is invaluable to debugging problems in an environment.

Request identifiers should be included that allow you to trace a request through all of the backend service calls made, so that the full request/response is available for the original request and any sub-requests made.

Once the logs are sent to a central service, metrics can be created from the logs. For example, the number of errors can be tracked per minute and alerts created. The number of logins or other transactions can be tracked and anomaly detection can be used to alert on strange behavior such as too many or too few.

The log metrics and alerts are the primary advantage of structured logging treated as an event stream. Metrics are useful for forensic telemetry analysis or capacity planning. Alerts should only be added for urgent human-actionable events. Avoid too many alerts that are not actionable as this can lead to alert fatigue on the team and missing of important alerts that require attention.

Practice using the central logging tool to find information quickly when there is no emergency going on, so that when the emergency does occur you will be able to use the tool effectively to identify problems.

Access to Production

On January 4, 2023, CircleCI reported that their software was breached by a malicious unauthorized third party. The breach happened because one of the CirclCI engineers installed some software on their laptop that contained some malware. This malware was able to hijack a valid, 2FA-backed SSO session. This session gave the bad actor production access to CircleCI's internal systems.

This allowed the actor to exfiltrate customer data out of the system by using this engineer's access level.

Security of customer data is extremely important to the business. In this incident, CircleCI was not attacked using an external vector, but they were attacked from within by one of their own engineer's accounts.

Similar attacks have been in the news lately where bad actors are using dependency tool chain attacks to get malicious code onto developer laptops or IDEs to hijack authenticated sessions.

Preventing these attacks requires us to prevent our internal staff from accessing production environments. If these types of attacks are to be prevented, no employee should have the ability to directly log into a production machine or directly query a production database.

Since the primary use case for this type of access is deployment, migrations, and debugging, the platform needs to address these concerns.

Deployment needs to be done using a service role which can only be assumed by the delivery pipeline. Data migrations should only be done using migration tools, such as alembic, laravel migrate, or liquibase, run from the delivery pipeline. This also ensures that all data changes are peer reviewed, and auditable.

Good, centralized logging should remove the need to log into any production server. If data store inspection is required, access to a read-only replica or copy should be granted on a temporary basis using some kind of zero-trust VPN solution, and revoked as soon as the investigation is completed.

If the disposability rule is followed, any problem process (low disk space, etc) should be able to be dealt with by terminating the process and launching a new one to replace it.

XII - Admin Processes

Administrative tasks have a similar concern around production access. The twelve factor app admin processes run as one-off processes in a production deployment.

There should never be a manual process run by someone logging into a production server. Instead, a migration tool like alembic or laravel migrate can be used to run these kinds of arbitrary scripts and ensure they are only run once per environment.

These migrations run within a deployment, and so they have access to the application codebase and environment configuration. These administrative scripts need to be committed to the repository and follow the same safety process such as peer review.

For any administrative task that needs to be run regularly a function or container can be created that can be parameterized and manually triggered to run in the cloud console. Proper permissions and roles can be granted to users who should be able to run these processes.

Invisible DevOps Discipline

Doing all of these things may seem overwhelming at first, but this is about intentionality and discipline. Take one thing at a time and incrementally improve your process and skills. Implement tooling to help check your code for common problems. Implement best practices such as reusable infrastructure or application code to make it easy to do the right thing.

Implementing all of these developer discipline practices will make it much easier to implement a fast, reliable, high quality delivery pipeline.

Chapter References

Wiggins, Adam. *The Twelve-Factor App.* 12factor.net/12factor.epub. Accessed April, 2022

Horowitz, Ben. *MRA, Part 5: Adapting the Twelve-Factor App for Microservices.* nginx.com/blog/microservices-reference-archit ecture-nginx-twelve-factor-app. Accessed April, 2022

CircleCI incident report for January 4, 2023 security incident. circleci.com/blog/jan-4-2023-incident-report/. Accessed Feb, 2023

Invisible DevOps

7 - High Quality Delivery Pipeline

The value delivery pipeline is probably the most important component of the *Invisible DevOps* system, and can be difficult for teams to do well.

One of the main reasons teams struggle with this is due to one or more of the development discipline practices discussed in Chapter 6 is not working well. Each of these practices contribute to a delivery pipeline that is safe and efficient.

Before work items even make it to the development team, the delivery pipeline is in use. The team is having conversations with the customer to get feedback on recent iterations and learn new ways the customer wants to use the product.

All of these conversations end up in an options list or backlog. The typical options list will have up to 30% or more work that will never be done by the team. This is why it's referred to as the options list and not a todo list. When adding to the options list, don't add a lot of detail or spend much time on this work item since it may never be worked on.

The more probable a work item in the options list will be worked on, the more detail can be added. The main detail required is how to know when the work item is done. This is usually called acceptance criteria. The acceptance criteria describes what needs to be true for the customer to consider this work item done.

Work items that the team is about to pick up should also be discussed by the team to determine if the card can be made any smaller. The goal is to make little bets on the value being delivered. The agile principle of simplicity is at work here: we need to maximize the amount of work **not** done.

Find the smallest slice of value that can be delivered to the customer to make a little bet. Show the customer and get feedback. You might find that the customer has no use for this feature, and save yourself a lot of time and effort. The customer may also want to make significant changes to what you would have delivered. Making little bets by splitting work items down to the minimum we can deliver saves time and allows us to be faster at delivering what the customer actually wants, not just faster at delivery.

The value delivery pipeline is a part of the platform product that moves code from developer environments to production environments. The goal of the delivery pipeline is to provide the team a high degree of confidence that their applications will work when moved into production. It accomplishes this by using a series of environments, rules, and automated tests. The pipeline must function as quickly as possibly while maintaining safety and quality.

Pipeline Orchestration

The value delivery pipeline is orchestrated by a pipeline orchestration tool. These tools will receive events from the repository when code is pushed and can begin the pipeline.

Github is a popular source repository tool If your organization is using github to store code, you might want to look at Github Actions as your pipeline orchestration tool. CircleCI and AWS CodePipeline are other orchestration tools commonly used, and there are many others out there.

The tool should be configured simply with as few environments as necessary and as much automation as possible.

The pipeline should be triggered on a commit to the mainline branch, such as master or main.

Environments

Environments are cloud accounts which can be deployed to. The recommended best practice is to place each environment in a separate cloud account. Cloud accounts provide a cost and security boundary. This makes it easier to track and reduce the cost of each environment, and to control access to environments based on roles.

If your organization has multiple products, each product should also be in its own cloud account per environment, separate from other products. Products should communicate with each other over public facing interfaces only, never through back-channel peered connections.

There should be at least three environments in your pipeline, although you may have more. These are development, test, and production. The development environment cloud account should provide developers with wide access permissions (with any appropriate guardrails) so that they can test services and deployments.

The test environment is the first environment deployed by the delivery pipeline. Development teams should not have read-only access to this cloud account. All deployments must be done through the delivery pipeline so that the deployment itself can be tested before being done in production.

The production environment is deployed last after all testing is completed. This is the environment used by your customers.

Test Automation

In addition to the developer discipline practices discussed in Chapter 6, there is one more that is critical for a great delivery pipeline: automated testing. Unit tests are run in the build environment as part of the delivery pipeline. The build environment is an isolated environment and so all tests run during build need to have backing services mocked.

Unit Tests

In a debate hosted at the 2007 JAOO conference, Bob Martin made the bold statement that developers are unprofessional and irresponsible if they do not practice unit test driven development (TDD).

As often happens with opinionated people, I don't always agree with Bob Martin. I want to take a very pragmatic stance on this topic.

Under the DevOps mindset we are to have a relentless focus on the customer and delivering value to the customer as quickly and safely as possible. There is a balance here. The definition of "safely" will vary depending on your industry. Some industries are developing software that is critical to the health of a patient in a medical setting. Some industries are providing less life-impacting entertainment news. These two settings will have a very different definition of "safety".

Using your industry requirements as a guide, we need to balance the value of automated testing against our delivery flow. Automated testing should provide confidence in our delivery pipeline allowing us to deliver faster and more frequently. However, the more tests we have, the slower our build and pipeline will be. There needs to be a pragmatic balance between these concerns and focus on writing only high value tests.

As Jim Coplien points out in the debate with Bob Martin, when using TDD, your unit test code mass will be about the same size as your application code mass. This also means that since we're writing 2x more code (application + test code), we should expect our flow to be cut in half with TDD.

Since all code contains bugs, there will be bugs in your application code as well as in your testing code. 100% unit test code coverage does not mean that the software is bug free and functions properly for the user.

Part of the reason for this is because there tends to be a mismatch between the level of abstraction of many unit tests and the level of abstraction of features. Since customers care only about features and not units, our testing should favor a higher level of abstraction where possible.

In general practice, we're supposed to write unit tests to test components in strict isolation as small units. However, features are not units rather features are found in the integration of units. Our users care about features and not units.

Should we throw out TDD then? I don't think so, but we do need to think about our testing at the right level of abstraction for the code we are about to write. We need to test what the user cares about.

Focus on keeping the speed of the test runs very quick, so that developers can run the tests frequently in the development environment and the tests do not slow down the build step in the delivery pipeline.

Contract Tests

In general contract testing is meant to ensure that the public interface remains consistent and does not introduce any breaking changes. These tests are especially important when different teams are working on components that need to communicate together.

These components might be different classes in the same system, or different services separated across the Internet. Contract tests are run in both the calling code and the dependency code to ensure both parties are adhering to the same agreed public interface contract.

Since all unit tests should be written against the public interface only, it is practical to perform contract testing as part of your unit testing strategy, rather than having separate contract tests. Unit tests can be written to watch for the following breaking changes in a public interface:

- Renaming any part of the interface contract, either the inputs or the outputs, properties or methods
- Reformatting any input or output properties, such as date formats
- Requiring any new input property that is not optional
- Removing any output property that was previously sent
- Removing any input method
- Requiring the caller to have an additional dependency, or context, or change the order of calls
- Requiring the caller to do anything differently when calling this contract

Note that we need to keep the robustness principle in mind with all public interfaces. We should be lenient in what the component accepts and strict in what it produces. Any extra parameters sent as inputs should be completely ignored. Required input formats should be as wide open as practical. We should not output any more fields than is absolutely necessary and we should provide a consistent, strict formatting to all output fields.

Similarly, test mocks for backing services can validate that the component under test is making appropriate calls to backing services which honor the interface contract. Such as sending data in the correct format, not including extra input fields, providing all required input fields, etc.

If contract testing is incorporated in the unit testing strategy, we don't need to add the complexity of separate contract tests.

Additionally, if the logging discipline practice is followed from Chapter 6, our production logs will contain events of all calls between services including all of the non-sensitive request parameters and response values. We can sample these request logs periodically and validate that the components running in the production or test environment are still honoring the interface contracts to ensure backward compatibility.

Integration Tests

While traditional unit testing tries to isolate the component under test, integration testing seeks to test the interaction between two components. These tests tend to be higher value than unit tests. The reason, as already mentioned, is because features exist as integrations between components, not as isolated units.

Since users care about features, we need to care more about integrations than individual units. When we start to write a feature that exists as an integration between components, the unit tests we write first need to be integration tests.

Integration tests should be written just like other unit tests. We need to mock all the backing services and test the integration of our component with a test double of the component being integrated with. This isolates the component under test and the backing service or component being integrated with.

Integration testing feels very similar to contract testing and it is. The difference is that integration tests are trying to validate the behavior of the application under test, while contract tests are validating that the communication between the components doesn't violate the public interface contract. Both types of unit tests are important to ensure correctness and compatibility.

Carefully written integration tests which use test doubles and validate the contract between components can run quickly in a build environment without the integrated component running. This allows you to perform more integration testing and ensure components are communicating correctly. Since features are the integrations, you might have more of these fast integration tests than isolated unit tests.

You will have to periodically update your test doubles if the public interface of dependent services gains new methods or inputs. This can be done when you want to use a newer version of the dependency interface.

Your test suite should have mostly integration and contract tests. Then fill in any missing code coverage with unit testing, avoiding duplicating any scenarios already covered by the integration tests.

End to End Tests

End to end testing is the only type of testing that is done against a running environment rather than during the build or development process.

These tests will use a test client to simulate user actions against the deployed application in a test environment.

The challenge with this type of testing is the volatility in the application under test. Nearly every single feature will include some changes to the user interface and so end to end tests are extremely time consuming to keep up to date.

End to end testing should therefore focus on testing extremely high value features for the business. Generally this should test the core product function on the happy path. End to End testing should not try to duplicate any existing integration or contract tests, but rather focus on testing the user interface.

These tests are the most difficult to write and maintain since the user interface is the most volatile component of the system and changes very frequently. Therefore write as few of these types of tests as possible.

Smoke Testing

Smoke testing is a form of end to end testing. However the purpose of smoke testing is to validate the deployment itself, rather than the application.

This type of testing should validate that all the required services are healthy in an environment. Smoke testing should also verify that extremely critical functionality is working, such as user login.

Testing Guideline

Unit tests should follow these guidelines:

- Only write unit tests from the perspective of a caller using the public interface. Do not directly test private implementation details.

- Write all unit tests with the contract in mind, to validate that new code does not introduce any breaking changes in the public interface
- Be sure to think about the input contract as well as the output contract. Avoid breaking changes in both.
- Mock all backing services using dependency injection so that tests can be run quickly in a build environment without access to backing services
- Focus on high value testing of likely inputs, error conditions, and malicious attack vectors rather than exhaustive fuzz testing.
- Perform integration testing using test doubles and focus on the behavior of the component as well as ensuring the component is honoring the interface contract when making calls.
- As Guillermo Rauch said, "write tests. Not too many. Mostly integration." -- your integration tests generally "contain" the unit tests.

- Start by writing integration tests, check code coverage, and fill in the gaps with unit tests.

Deployment Tool

The tool that deploys, and sometimes builds the assets that are being deployed in each environment is called a deployment tool. Many common language frameworks will include deployment tools that can be used to build, test, and deploy code and configuration to an environment.

Some examples of deployment tools are AWS CDK, SAM and Amplify, serverless.com, sst.dev, laravel forge, etc.

It is a good idea to use the deployment tool that comes with your language framework whenever possible.

Putting the Pipeline Together

Let's put all of this information together into a cohesive delivery pipeline.

The Development Environment

The development environment is a combination of a local environment, such as the developer's laptop, and a development cloud account.

The developers should have broad access to the development cloud account. This allows them to test various services and test their deployments. Guardrails should be set up in this account to prevent unwanted behavior such as using unwanted regions.

Where possible, cloud managed services should be used rather than simulated in a local environment. This will eliminate any differences in the behavior of these services, especially access control.

Developers may work on feature branches or work in a more continuous integration fashion using trunk based development. Peer review and product owner acceptance testing can occur in this environment before pushing the code to the mainline branch when it is potentially shippable to production.

Code linting or other static analysis checks can be configured as branch protections on the mainline branch if desired.

The pipeline generally starts with a push to the mainline branch of the repository. This triggers the orchestration tool.

The Build Environment

The build environment is the first step in the process after code is pushed to the mainline. This environment generally lives within the orchestration tool you are using. For example CircleCI hosts build containers that will run your build process.

The build will compile your code into deployable assets and run your unit, integration, and contract tests. The build environment will not have any backing services, so these tests must include mocks and test doubles for these.

The test suite must reside within the codebase for the application, so that the build environment will have the test suite when it checks out the code from the mainline branch.

The compile process and test suite should be made to run as fast as possible.

Once the build succeeds and the tests pass, the orchestration tool moves the code to the test environment.

The Test Environment

The test environment should only be modified by the deployment tool run inside the pipeline orchestration tool. Developers should not have write access to the cloud account for this environment to ensure it remains in a consistent state.

The test environment is the first environment that is deployed with the automated tooling. This is why the automated tooling should be used only, and no manual deployments. This allows this environment to test the deployment process itself.

If there is a schema or data migration tool being used, this should run first, before the code is deployed. Recall from Chapter 6 that these schema migrations need to be backward compatible since the old code will still be running for a time after the migrations are done.

If the migrations are successful, then the deployment tool is run to deploy the code to the test environment. The tool will need to have credentials for the cloud environment to operate. These credentials are secrets that are configured in your orchestration tool.

Once the code is deployed, the smoke tests and end to end tests can be run against the test environment. These tests also need to reside in the application code repository, so the orchestration tool has them available to run.

At this point, there are two options for the pipeline. If your team has a high confidence in your testing process through peer reviews and automated testing then code can automatically be moved to production at this point if the tests pass.

If the team doesn't have very good automated testing yet and has a low confidence in the quality process, there might be a manual approval gate here in the pipeline to allow for manual exploratory testing and validation before moving the code to production.

The Production Environment

As soon as the test environment tests pass, or the pipeline is manually approved, the orchestration tool can run the deployment tool against the production environment.

Once again, schema and data migrations are run first, and then the code is deployed, followed by the smoke tests again. End to end tests are not run in production.

Like the test environment, developers should not have write access to the production environment. Only the automated tooling should be allowed to make changes to production.

One of the most common reasons developers want access to production is to debug issues using logs, inspect data to diagnose bugs, and to fix data that has become corrupted. Following the advice in Chapter 6, high quality, low noise logs will be available in a central location for use in debugging. Any data changes should be made only by the automated process with a migration tool.

Developers should be given a facility to temporarily gain access to a read-only copy of the production data for investigations. This might be a read replica or a database copy, but should not be the production write instance. Even read only access can cause performance issues and outages in a production write instance.

High Quality Delivery Pipeline

The steps and environments described above can result in a high quality delivery pipeline that gives your team confidence to ship code fast and safe.

Writing high value automated testing is critical to this process. Testing in the same way the user will interact with the components by favoring integration tests will give a higher confidence in the quality of the product.

Having the pipeline run fast and completely automated will allow you to move code into production faster. This will enable the team to write smaller iterations of code with higher quality. Faster iterations allows for more feedback from the user to drive future iterations.

Chapter References

Jim Coplien and Bob Martin Debate TDD. youtube.com/watch?v=KtHQGs3z. Accessed April, 2022

Fowler, Martin. *IntegrationTest.* martinfowler.com/bliki/IntegrationTest.html. Accessed April, 2022

Sims, Peter. *Little Bets: How Breakthrough Ideas Emerge from Small Discoveries.* Free Prees. 2011.

8 - The Invisible DevOps System

This book describes the *Invisible DevOps* system. The system is a framework of components. Each component might be implemented differently by different organizations depending on their circumstances.

Following the *Invisible DevOps* system will help to reduce waste, increase quality and increase flow of value delivered to customers.

Step One - Organizational Mindset

The first step is to educate the organization on the benefits and principles of the DevOps culture and mindset: Respecting People, Continuous Improvement, Optimize the Whole, Focus on Customers, Enhance Learning, Empower your Team, Increase Flow, and Build Quality In.

This is the foundation of the *Invisible DevOps* system. DevOps should be invisible in an organization because it becomes "just the way we do things around here".

This should be a top-down adoption of DevOps principles requiring buy-in from the executive team. If you are selling this to your executives, focus on the value of DevOps, the value of moving quicker and safer and learning from the customers. DevOps is not a cost center in an organization, but a culture of operating that reduces waste, increases quality, and saves the company money.

If you find yourself in an organization that is struggling to understand the value of devops then start with a small team of DevOps minded developers. Show the organization what's possible to achieve with the *Invisible DevOps* framework.

Step Two - Team Structure

Evaluate your team structure. Use Conway's law to justify any reorganizations that are required. Organize teams so that they are constrained by Conway's Law to produce the ideal architecture for your product.

If you have only a single team and a single product, then use this part of the framework to plan for future growth. Begin thinking of what growth would look like and how multiple teams would contribute to the product. Identify complicated subsystems or isolated sub-products that could become owned by a second team.

Always plan for the next stage of company growth so that when it becomes necessary, the architecture and organization structure will be ready.

Step Three - Continuous Improvement

Begin putting in place a system for continuous improvement. Document how projects should be run such as goals, measurements, timeboxing, and how they will be documented and communicated.

Plan, Do, Check, Act, Repeat. Keep a list of experiments waiting to be done and make steady improvement over time. Communicate successes to build confidence in the process.

The first rounds of improvement might be related to treating the platform as a product.

Step Four - The Platform as a Product

Even with small teams it is important to start thinking of the platform as a product. This product supports your application and provides it with certain qualities.

The main components of this platform are: delivery pipeline, deployment tools, migration tools, infrastructure code, log aggregation, debugging tools, development environment, audit logging, monitoring, alerting, shared infrastructure, and more.

The main goal of the platform product is to make the right way to do application development be the easy way. The platform should make it difficult to implement anti-patterns or break through guardrails.

Step Five - Embrace Cloud Paradigms

Review your application's usage of the cloud and identify places where the cloud could be leveraged more by the application.

Does your application have enough redundancy or scalable capacity to meet user demand trends? Is your application data encrypted in transit and at rest? Are you taking advantage of managed services and serverless products to reduce vulnerability and patch management efforts?

Review your security posture in the cloud to ensure that roles and permissions are granted using least privilege and can be justified by business need. Create "break glass" mechanisms for developers or other staff to fix an environment by hand if necessary. Ensure that usage of these "break glass" measures are logged in a central audit log.

Put in place a cost and performance optimization program that will track cost and usage to create the right balance for the application.

Step Six - Discipline Practices

Begin to implement the developer discipline practices in an intentional way. These practices are intended to create high quality, resilient applications that can easily be deployed into a cloud environment.

Use the twelve factor app as a shared language for talking about and understanding these disciplines.

The most important of these is backwards compatibility, disposability and idempotency. These allow for a safe delivery pipeline to be created. All of these practices are important to create a culture of DevOps in your organization.

Step Seven - The Delivery Pipeline

Create a high quality, fast delivery pipeline. Putting all the developer discipline practices in place allows for this pipeline to deliver code with zero downtime.

Having high quality automated tests brings confidence in automating the delivery pipeline all the way through to production. This allows your team to move quickly and develop in small iterations to get fast feedback from the customer.

Invisible DevOps

Putting all of these components into practice in your organization will put you ahead of the

DevOps curve. Organizations that treat DevOps as an invisible culture get the most benefit out of DevOps.

If you already have a "DevOps team" or "DevOps engineer" in your organization, consider breaking down the silos and putting them in the development teams, or turning them into the "platform team" to iterate on the platform as a product.

Nothing in the *Invisible DevOps* system requires a complete overhaul of your organization's practices, tools, or code. Rather this is a process of continuous improvement that should never end for your organization.

Following the Plan-Do-Check-Act framework, start small and pick one component to implement at a time. Identify targets and metrics to measure progress. Celebrate successes and improvement goals met.

Steady, continuous improvement is more valuable in the long run than large sweeping organizational changes.

This is the *Invisible DevOps* system.